IMPERIAL YOUTH REVIEW #2

EDITED BY
CHRIS KELSO &
GARRETT COOK

T0315994

Published by
Dog Horn Publishing
45 Monk Ings, Birstall, Batley WF17 9HU
United Kingdom
doghornpublishing.com

Edited by
Chris Kelso and Garrett Cook

ISBN 978-1-907133-81-7

Cover design by
Daniele Serra

Typesetting by
Jonathan Penton

UK Distribution: Central Books
99 Wallis Road, London, E9 5LN, United Kingdom
orders@centralbooks.com
Telephone:+44 (0) 845 458 9911
Fax: +44 (0) 845 458 9912

Overseas Distribution: Printondemand-worldwide.com
9 Culley Court
Orton Southgate
Peterborough
PE2 6XD
Telephone: 01733 237867
Fax 01733 234309

Imperial Youth Review #2

TABLE OF CONTENTS

Paperback
978-1-84694-678-3
$18.95 | £9.99
216x140 mm
264pp.

eBook
978-1-84694-526-7
$9.99 | £6.99

US Distribution:
National Book Netwo

UK Distribution:
Orca Marston

perfectedgebooks.com

PERFECT
EDGE
BOOKS

It's been rough lately for the Lord of Darkness, with ex-girlfriend drama rearing its head at inconvenient moments, ancient gods returning to take over the universe, and Satan's own unstoppable laziness. But whatever. Satan is okay, and he thinks you're okay, too. This whole eternal damnation thing is all a bit of a misunderstanding. He runs Hell as a resort, kind of. A vacation spot. The point is, he's not a bad guy. He's trying to save Heaven and all of creation, and he only has a dimwitted giant, a surly waitress, and a monkey to help him. So, a thank you might be nice. Maybe buy him a cup of coffee next time you see him. And you will see him. It's the Apocalypse, and all that.

Michael Paul Gonzalez lives in Los Angelese. michaelpaulgonzalez.com

INTRODUCTION:
CHRIS KELSO IS A PRETENTIOUS WANKER
by Chris Kelso

I'm in hospital right now, but I remember…

…Walking around the corner and turning into my local pub – a run-down shite-hole called "The Wifebeater". You get an eclectic bunch in here usually. I see Cleary, the local head banger sipping froth from his pint. He sees me and waves me over. Cleary is in an art-rock band called "Fuck Almighty". They perform demonstrations and are fairly political – they're also completely shite. That's not the point though…apparently.

- Alright my old son – he says.

Cleary is a good 5 years my junior, it annoys me when he calls me "son". He knows I'm a writer and likes to undermine me.

- Any gigs? – I ask disparagingly. His face drains of all colour.
- No. Nothing yet.
- Ach well, chin up.

Inside I'm smiling like a smug bastard. A cell phone glows through Cleary's jeans. He excuses himself to take the call.

At that moment, Danny Mclean has arrived – a man of unwholesome proclivity – the local nutter. A pale fear overcomes me. The last time he was here he killed a man, a man called Archibald. They say Archibald's head was so beaten up that it went completely black, septic black.

Anyway, McLean is pretty untouchable, seeing as how his wee brother is a copper. He's a bald, squat specimen with no visibly obvious presence, but his reputation precedes him. His face is a map of scars, a series of fresh cuts overlapping on his left cheek. I turn to the counter and order a pint of Fosters, trying to ignore the mental cunt who's just entered. That's the thing about "The Wifebeater", I only come here because I appear more intelligent and successful than the regular clientele, but when murderers and thugs start popping in for a swift-half it sets me on edge, makes me question my strategy. Cleary sits back down on the stool beside me, his ridiculous poodle haircut wilting at the fringe. He looks anguished.

- What's the matter with your face? – I ask.

- That was my bloody guitarist 'Roach'. He's got meningitis. How typical is that?

- Bloody typical aye.

'Roach' is a stupid name for a guitarist.

- A week before the big gig at Spoons.

- Chin up, maybe mental Mclean will fill in for ye.

I don't know why I said it.

I am prone to moments of reckless abandon when in the company of people I feel superior to.

- Here, I think he heard ye…

Christ, please don't have let him hear me. I swivel on the stool and see him coming towards me.

FUCK.SAKE

- Alright big man – he says eyeing my profile up and down.

- Aye…

- You're wee Chrissy Kelso, ain't ye?

- Aye…

- Heard you were writing wee books n' that…

- Aye…

- Well excuse me if ah don't ask for yer autograph big man. Christ sake, ah could write a book if ah wanted to!

- Course you could, it'd probably be better than mine!

Self-deprecation is wasted on this head case. I adopt an apologetic tone.

- Look, Danny, I'm really…

- Yer really what? Really sorry? Ye fuckin should be wearing that scarf!

Everyone in the pub laughs on cue. Mclean grabs a fistful of my scarf and lassos me in until I'm inches from his gin soaked, scar-ridden face.

- You no from Cumnock?

- Originally from Cumnock aye.

- Well then why the fuck are you comin into this pub dressed like a fuckin poofter?

I don't know what to say. I *am* from Cumnock, but I'm keen to dispel that factoid around biographers and journalists.

I'm terrified of confrontation. Mental Mclean has illuminated something I'd previously failed to resolve in myself, an intrinsic flaw of the personality.

I really am a pretentious cunt to these people.

Danny untightens his grip on my scarf and with one swift motion tears it free of my neck. He wraps it round his head like Rambo's bandana, limping his wrist and adopting a feminine accent (which I believe was meant to be an impression of me). My humiliation made complete when Danny decides to get out his cock and balls and proceed to dip them in my pint of Fosters.

I'm overwhelmed by a need to fight back, defend myself. It's the Imperial Youth VS the Antiquated Brutish Old BASTARD…

I have the backing of some of the greatest young minds of our generation, of any generation!

I pick up my pint glass and toss the pissy beer over Danny Mclean's hideous mug…

IMPERIAL YOUTHS ASSEMBLE!!!!

I am now in hospital…

Chris Kelso *is the editor of* Imperial Youth Review, *author and illustrator.*

BEARDS

by Michael A Rose

INTRODUCTION:
SWEET MERCIFUL FUCK, THERE'S AN ISSUE TWO
by Garrett Cook

Well. Fuck. Holy shit. We made a magazine. It's a good magazine too. There were a lot of people who said we couldn't do it, but...

Shit. That's a lie. Nobody said we couldn't do it. This project has been blessed with love and support and passion from the getgo. Nobody said no. Nobody said "fuck you" or "show me the money". By the way, we're working on that. This mag costs an arm and a leg, but it's still what some people pay for a takeaway burger. And unlike McEvil, we won't feed you crap.

Every time I turn around, someone puts hand to brow and says "reporting for duty". So, Issue 2. We got so much support and so many subs for Issue 1 that we barely had to get any new material for two.

The love is exploding. And if you, dear reader come around for Issue 3, you'll be seeing plenty of gooey, pulsating juicy meaty bloody tasty love. But the Issue in your hands is a great one. Full of talent, full of exuberance and because I moved female contributors forward to Issue 1 from the getgo, full of testosterone.

Sweet merciful fuck, we made a magazine. We made a blog where contributors can do as they please, we made safe places to transgress and a haven for love, friendship and revolution. We're not as big as we could be, but I'm proud and happy and shocked to bring you Issue 2.

We're great is what we are.

Garrett Cook is the fucking editor of this fucking magazine.

SPEAK OF THE DEVIL
by Don Webb

The devil rears his head in many guises. He's there when a teenage Satanist yells the Infernal Names from the *Satanic Bible*, He's there when the pious Yezidi calls upon the Peacock Angel, he there in Scottish curses ("May the Devil walk behind ye!"), and he is there in resplendent glory in the works of George Bernard Shaw, Anatole France, Mark Twain and Robert Irwin. He shows up as a tempter, a trickster, a friend of man, a merciless accuser. He is in myriads of cultures – sometimes holistically part of the pantheon among American Indians and West Africans, sometimes a culture hero in Greece, a Patron of rulers for the Aztecs and some Egyptians. He can be a She with names like Hecate, Asarte or Kali. The devil reflects both what we fear and long for. Let's look at his trappings and Names, and see what He mirrors for mankind, and as a bonus I will throw in a powerful Invocation that 99% of you would be scared to ever utter.

We'll start with trappings. The Devil is said to appear if spoken of. He loves Midnight and cross-roads. Humans recognize the power of darkness in their lives. It may be well integrated in powerful humans who use their dark side – Pride, Aggression, Desire – to achieve their wants. This aspect of the Devil was well-charted by Ayn Rand's writings on greed or by Jung's writings on the Shadow. But many humans are run by their dark side rather than running it. Addiction, cruelty, aggression make the human different than other animals. We disturb the natural order. Look at our species at its worst and you will not mistake man for something as noble as a wolf or humming bird. But look at our art, our music, our strivings of the mind and once again we see that something is different about humans. We know that this difference is always there, a secret hidden in every heart, so we fear calling it forth. The Devil is always very near. He loves Midnight for three reasons. First Midnight is the sign of potential in time. It is that moment when today becomes yesterday tomorrow becomes today. Today is the place of action where we have the greatest freedom (but feel most enslaved). Tomorrow is the home of our desires and dreams. Tomorrow is the unmanifest, from which we call all things. Yesterday is the repository of advice and momentum. Because of the way we keep time in the West, Midnight alone touches these three magical realms. Its significance can be felt by anyone – even the least magical human you know is overcome with this triune mystery every New Year's Eve. The second reason that the Devil loves Midnight is that it is a time when human beings are acting on their own schemes. Unlike the healthy light of the workaday world – midnight is a time for lovers, dreamers, revolutionaries and thieves. Lastly the Devil loves Midnight for magical reasons. If you want to change consensus reality, you will have greater luck when most of the humans around you are asleep. Now to a large extent we realize (as Gurdjieff did) that most humans are asleep all of the time, but the time of physical sleep is when most humans shut down the top structures of their brains and allow their old brains to reprogram based on the day's data (I will write about this phenomenon more in a later article). The Devil loves cross roads for two reasons. Firstly they represent places of decision. The archetype of the Devil is about making the decision that goes against the grain of the world – what place more than a cross-road asks the question "Where do you want to go?" And you may rest assured that the Devil takes the stand of poet Robert Frost on this one. But cross roads have a secondary meaning as well. They are places where you can meet people unexpectedly. The synchronicity of meeting the right person at the right time is wrapped in the archetype of demonic initiation. As humans we can draw on three sources of models to make our decisions. We can draw on our own experience, we can draw on the experiences of the people around us (our family, our culture), and lastly we call upon recorded experience – we read about it, we saw the movie. But when we meet a new human we can be inspired by his or her experience. Even a short meeting with as gifted teacher or a culture hero (or villain) can open all sorts of possibilities to a human. Oedipus lost his lot by slaying the man (his father) he met in a cross roads. If one can be open to the new, as a source of perspective one is open to Prometheus stolen fire or Satan's apple. Combine these three archetypes and you will find the Devil easy to call up. Let's look at some of His names and see Him as an archetype of human experience.

Hecate. The dark Greek goddess evolved in an unusual fashion. In her oldest form she was associated with cross roads, thresholds and boundaries. This is a symbol of the human psyche – ever considering what it is and what is beyond it – as well as it what its rules are and when to transgress them. Hecate became a literary figure next. Most modern witches assume that classical writers that made Hecate into the patron of sorcery were coping from tradition. In fact her literary reputation came first and from this she became the witches' friend. Art is a great key for the Devil. Lastly she became Hecate *Soteira* –Hecate the Savior. She became a symbol of the world-soul – for the Elect she was the "tender hearted" model of how the individual soul may advance. This is a logical progression form physical liminality to a sorcerous temptress (see the Devil and Midnight and cross roads) to finally the symbol of one who having mastered the power to disturb the universe uses that power to order and immortalize her own soul. There are different explanations of her name; I tend to trust the etymology that connects her with a Greek word for "will."

Coyote. Culture hero and Trickster, Coyote is known to a number of American Indian tribes. (My Chickasaw ancestors preferred Rabbit for this role.) Claude Levi-Struass theorized that Coyote place as a Trickster came from his role as a mediator between life and death. He has powers of shapeshifting and resurrection. Both of these deny the natural order. In the natural order, everything has a place and a fate to be fulfilled. The shapeshifter transcends this order, and not obeying the most primal law of all – death – marks Coyote as a creature whose possibilities point beyond the laws of the well-regulated universe.

Prometheus. Like Coyote, Prometheus steals fire from the gods and gives it to man. This is an especaially telling act. Prometheus is not all powerful like Zeus, he must steal from Zeus to gain power. In this he is already the double of humans. Because he gave fire to humans, Zeus punished him by binding him to rock cliff where an eagle ate his liver every day. He also possess a power that Zeus, supreme god of the natural order lacks, the power of prophecy. If the universe ran in a clockwork fashion, it would be easy to predict the outcome of things. But because free will is in the world (symbolized by the Divine Fire Prometheus gave to humans), prediction is an art. Zeus fearful of his own fate has his half-human son Hercules free Prometheus in exchange for prophecy. In ancient Greece a Left Hand Path cult of Prometheus wore iron rings to remind themselves both of Prometheus' bondage and freedom. He is not as powerful as the Gods, but he can outwit them – much like his human relative Odysseus.

Eblis. The Devil of Islam's name means "he that causes despair." For the Sufi Ayn al-Qozat Hamadani wrote that Eblis created the condition of separation from Allah. He has a special affinity for separated ones, those who choose separation rather than union. In his admirable book *Sacred Drift*, Peter Lamborn Wilson writes

> Ayn al-Qozat implies that separation-in-love is in some sense superior to union-in-love, because the former is a dynamic condition and the later a static one. Eblis is not only the paragon of separated ones, he also causes the same condition in human lovers – and although some experience this as "evil," the Sufi knows that this is necessary and even good.

Stephen Flowers in his *Lords of the Left Hand Path* points out that this seems to anticipate Aleister Crowley's *Book of the Law*, wherein Nuit says: "For I am divided for love's sake, for the chance of union." Eblis is the archetype of the path of non-union, the Left Hand Path.

Lilith. Adam's first wife became a demon by her own efforts. She is mythically the first human to immortalize herself and gain magical powers. She refused to accept a non-equal role to Adam, and survived Jehovah's displeasure at this rebellion. She is the face of the Devil hat teaches by standing against political oppression; one may achieve power both for one's self and one's cause. She is Nuit, pure and simple – her name comes from the Semetic root L-Y-L (Hebrew *layal* Night). Like Hecate she stands in for the Devil's love of Midnight. She is a major figure in many Wiccan traditions. Doreen Valiente says of this Craft Goddess that she is "the personification of erotic dreams, the suppressed desire for delights".

Saturn. The father of Jupiter is considered the personification of the Ordeal. All the things in our lives that are hard on us – poverty, old age, loss of loved ones – and so on are Saturn' domain. Saturn in his Greek name of Chronos is about the supreme challenge that humans face, time. We either bend it to our will, or we become logs on its endless fire. Yet Saturn is a strengthening figure. By meeting his challenges we become more and more ourselves. He is the mythological form of Nietzsche's much-quoted aphorism, "What does not kill me only makes me stronger." A German Left Hand Path group, the *Fraternitas Saturni*, chose Saturn as its god. This group led by Gregor A. Gregorius (Eugene Groshce) developed Crowley's philosophy of Will by idealizing the process of "overcoming" as the means by which the soul acquired both identity and immortality. Gregorius associated Saturn explicitly with Lucifer/Satan, and claimed he ruled a path of transformation. The Devil wants your empowerment. For an excellent view of Saturn in the Indian Left Hand Path see Robert Svoboda's excellent *The Greatness of Saturn*, which shows the transformation by Ordeals ruled over by Shani Dev.

Leviathan. In Hebrew Kabbalah this Devil's name is equal to 496, which is equal to Malkuth, the "kingdom" or in other words the physical world. Leviathan has a premier place in modern Satanism. In the 1897 book *La Clef de la Magie Noire*, Stanislas de Guaita created the Sigil of Baphomet. This is an inverse pentagram with the name Leviathan spelled out in Hebrew (LVIThN) counter clockwise with the "L" appearing beneath the lowest point. The serpent from Hebrew mythology becomes a symbol for the circling forces of time bounding the psyche (symbolized by the inverse pentagram). This is key to the initiatory life, if one becomes aware of (and finally Master) of the patterns that return (both within and without) in one's life – one changes the whole world (Malkuth) into an initiatory gymnasium – using both the challenges (Saturn) and the pleasures of life (Lilith/Kali) as means to becoming a more powerful immortal essence. The Sigil of Baphomet was chosen by Anton LaVey as the symbol of the Church of Satan. This led it to becoming *the* symbol of the Devil in countless movies, videos and rock albums. Almost everyone knows the sign but do not understand its meaning, which was made into a magical concept of *Remanifestation* by James Lewis of the Temple of Set, founder of the Order of Leviathan. This is true of real occult symbols, they may be seen everywhere. They rule the many and are ruled by the few. A secret has an effect on the manifested world.

Kali. This is one of the many names of the Goddess of Tantra. The Tantric path is about the use of the objects of desire as means to liberation. Rather than the austere Right Hand Path that seeks to elimante desire so that the soul can return in union to its source, the Tantrtic path uses desire as way for a soul to become a friend and equal to the gods. Both paths realize that the objects of desire are temporary. If you are unclear on this place a slice of key lime pie in your desk for a week. In Right Hand Path thought the key to be immortality is to turn one's sense away from these distractions and temptations. In Tantra, a path of indulgence rather than absence is required. One gains temporary unity with each desire and then inflames one's self to seek new experience in the cosmos. Kali, as the skull-girdled Destroyer of Worlds, personifies this process in her mad intoxicated dance. Re-crating pone's soul in this shape likewise moves from the impermanence of objects to permanence of spirit, but of an individual spirit dedicating to enjoying the cosmos.

Loki. Early etymologists connected his name with "Fire" but actually the Germanic Trickster's name means "the Ender." Odhin made Loki his blood-brother became he understood the need for reversals and trick endings. Loki is the flaw in any system that makes the system either evolve into a stronger, more permanent form or perish. It is noticebl that Loki's wife is Sygn, Victory (as in "Sig" of "Sig Heil!"). Victory in warfare and in life requires the quick wits and cunning of Loki – and often his jealousy as motivation. Loki is a shapeshifter, and is often pressed into the service of the gods – a role that Mephistopheles fulfills – remember he tells Faust, that he is part of that Power that "desires only Evil, but achieves only Good." Loki brings about the destruction of the world in order for a better stronger world to Remanifest.

We have looked at a few of the Devil's names, but what is the Devil's secret? It is a simple one. "Devil" spelled backwards is "Lived." The key to all "infernal" advice – using pleasure and pain, being crafty and giving of the secret of fire to others that your power may grow, resisting political oppression, predicting the future – is found on one place only. It is found not in books, nor in gurus, but in examining one's life. The text that the Devil suggests is neither a Bible nor a book of philosophy, but examining the contents of one's own life. The text of another is an affront to the self. The Devil is you – your experiences good and bad, complex and simple – they have led you on the path of non-union. Jung called this the path of individuation, the integration of the Shadow, accepting and learning from your Darkness leads you to creating your own light, your own unique Star.

An Invocation

Should you desire to meet the Devil, perform the invocation below. Write it out on a piece of parchment. On the opposite side draw an inverse pentagram and write the word DEVIL counter-clockwise at each point beginning with the lowest one. Read the invocation aloud at midnight at a cross-roads. When you are done lay it on the ground and put 93 pence non top of it. Go home by an indirect means. Tell no one of this for three days. Think long and hard about your life. You will meet the Devil.

"I speak the Devil's Name for I am a Faust seeking Mephistopheles. 'D' is for Diabolous, the truth of many Wills string together and in conflict in the Cosmos, "E" is for Eblis that teachs love-in-separation and makes me Desire the embrace of my Secret Soul, 'V' is for Vampire that teaches me to draw strength out of my enemies so that I will fight for my principles beyond death, 'I' is for Incubus that teaches I can summon pleasure form the Unmanifest, 'L' is for Leviathan that teaches that I will Remanifest in the glory of my Infernal Will. I have said that Names. I have Lived, so I am the Devil. In my own wisdom I will meet my hidden self. I leave 93 pennies for the guy."

Googlemania

To enjoy this article more, google the symbolism of 93, each of the Devil's names, the show "Poor Devil" on YouTube, the "Electric Preludes" on YouTube and an "Essay on Literary Satanism" by Don Webb.

Don Webb is an American science fiction and mystery writer, and former High Priest of the Temple of Set.

CLASSIFIED: INTERNET PORN

Recent classified government studies have shown that people between the ages of ten and seventy are likely to be ADDICTED TO INTERNET PORN. The insidious neurotransmitter known as dopamine rewires the porn addict's brain without him/her being aware of it. No sure-fire cure has been developed—till now! Visit tombradley.org.

Tip #1
Avoid drinking shots of Love.
The hangover is terrible.

This and other
Tips For Avoiding
can be found in
Avoiding Mortimer by J. W. Wargo

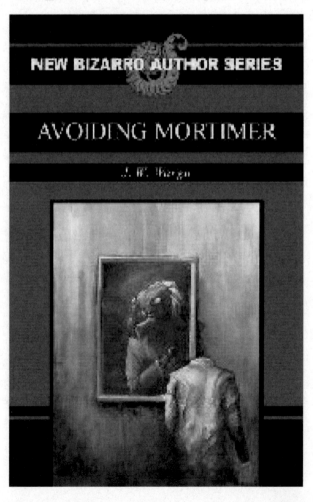

YOUR BARAGOUIN
by Jordan Krall

This is the time of moldy razors.

Puffs of inky smoke cover the ceiling, hiding the water stains and the insect trails under intangible codes of burning words. This is the last time the teacher will open a book.

This is the last time the teacher will teach.

The students lie on the floor, their old bones creaking and cracking, spilling white noise into the air. Their groans slither through the din and split sound waves into ancient languages. Consonants poke candent holes through the teacher's lesson. If there are vowels, they are hiding under the shroud of a guttural curriculum.

With a weak but determined hand, the teacher pours the remains of the book into the cup and drinks. Bathic blasphemy always soothes the throat like ancient tongues professing flowers and chalk dust. Black eggs split and sizzle in the teacher's stomach: a chamber of undigested commerce.

Speaking through multiple tongues, the teacher lifts several curses off the students, tearing their sweaty tendril-like thoughts out of the air and places them in jelly jars. Each top is screwed carefully as to not disturb the warm, obscene glass.

The teacher places each jar in a night table drawer. The night table itself has been crafted from broken and obscure texts. It was a gift from the teacher's father-in-law. The old man bought it in a crusty shop in a noisy town northwest of the school. It was meant to be a frivolous curio.

It is slowly becoming a gelatinous tomb.

The jars rattle and the night table shrieks in a morbid cacophony of exclamations and explanations. It shivers into blobs, falls to the hardwood floor, and surrounds the students who do not notice the creeping horror of the night table. The teacher mutters several words but knows the volume and tone are not sufficient to arouse the students from their raptus.

Crooked maps of outdated lands cover the walls in overlapping confusion of broken borders and obsidian lakes. The teacher points to a spot and asks a question. The only reply is a din of arrogant disappointment.

A leather case opens and a razor is removed.

The teacher's face droops in feminine folds, red sparks claiming a place near the breast, burning holes and giving birth to hungry oblivion. The aching holes contract and expand and contract and expand and squirt purplish corrective fluid across the eyes of the students.

Modifications are made and behaviors are adjusted.

Brazen gobs of drool spill out onto the floor and turn into historical shapes that envelope the students, transforming them into proud cocoons. Bags of teeth are removed from hidden pockets and the teeth are strewn across the room like yellow ruins of an archaic king.

Small bone twigs and totems of hair recreate battles, walking across the wall maps with purposeless poise. Caves amidst the mountain ranges ejaculate insects into the theatrical fracas. Fireworks of dust and boredom are vomited into the air, blinding the teacher.

In a matter of seconds, several things are learned. Several things are lost. Several things cease to exist.

Again: they cease to exist.

The memories slowly evaporate and are replaced with small jelly jars filled with sand and spittle. Time is simply corrected, erased and rewritten. The jars are quickly hidden in a night table drawer.

The nurse is sent for and she arrives in a huff.

She asks about the problem but before she can receive a reply she is bombarded by a spectrum of light and shadow, brilliance and boredom, expectations and disappointment buried in bulbous spirals that are being ejected from the teacher's cockeyed skull.

The nurse reacts accordingly. She takes out her leather case and slips a razor out. It shines in the spectrum, scattering the future across the wall maps. Borders become scum, spreading across inches, across miles of sheetrock and stale paint until the room is a microcosmic disaster.

All the fingernails in the room throw tantrums like small children, breaking away from their parents and spiting everyone, everything in their path. They join the teeth and soon the hair arrives, moving into throbbing clumps. They ache with anticipation. They smother the nurse's hand, slaughtering the razor in dark follicle movements.

The teacher screams.

Ceiling tiles fall and bring a deluge of year-old rainwater.

Molecular rapture implodes. Every heart in the room is enlarged. Egg white seeds splatter onto the teacher's nose. Pink noise escapes small puckered speakers that have been bolted inside the second drawer of the night table. Then primordial acoustics tremble, filling the room with sound waves birthed of ancient spinal cords and guttural languages that have been documented into a multitude of accursed curricula.

Strips of skin fall to the floor. They sizzle like bacon. The students crawl like worms and eat their knowledge. Both teacher and nurse act accordingly: they gather up their belongings, their razors, and leave town.

They relocate to the noisy town and shop for a new night table.

A new tomb.

Then: they cease to exist.

Jordan Krall *writes in various genres for various presses. He also runs Dynatox Ministries.*

HALF-SICK OF SHADOWS
by Edward Morris

I.

The small, fussy man in the gray disposable suit sat in a metal folding chair and wrung his hands at the bedside. His throat clicked when he swallowed. Beads of sweat guttered down his egg-shaped forehead.

Morty Stein always wore a disposable suit on Wednesdays. And gloves, too, good carbon-fiber exam gloves you couldn't even see. And a jock strap, and cellophane around his ass, wrapped double across his junk. (His Mamma didn't raise a *gonif.*)

But for some things, there was no sufficient amount of prep-work here. Not just now. With the mere paragraph she'd just spoken at him from her hospital bed, his client's daughter was about to drag him tooth-by-tooth across and down the jaws of every global media megalith there ever was, if any of this cluster-fuck ever leaked to the press.

He didn't have this coming. He always showed up for this, and more than this.

SP4 Morty Stein, United States Army (Ret., Hon.,Medical) had nearly sweated through the armpits of that day's suit. His ears were ringing in the circulated air. He was never more uncomfortable in his own skin than he was on that one Wednesday out of each and every month, just because of what he hoped he wouldn't find. But he came down there every Wednesday anyway.

Even this one. This Wednesday to end all Wednesdays.

Morty had no idea how he wound up anywhere. He'd worked for the firm of Acosta, Blomberg and Black since he was a year out of law school on the New GI Bill, with the ink still wet on his bar exam. They started him right at the bottom six years ago, and there was still no Stein anywhere on the firm's letterhead.

There were mitigating factors for this assignment, ones he hadn't seen until he was squarely in its mouth. When he was nineteen, Morty worked as an attendant at a day center for a 'profoundly developmentally-disabled population', as he was taught to say. An old science fiction novel by some guy named Terrance Dicks, which Morty once read on break at that gig, called those kinds of populations 'genetic wounded.' He liked that better.

But no matter how genetically wounded any of them were, Morty could always look in their eyes (while he was changing their adult diapers, or doing PT stuff with them, or flushing the feeding-tubes in their stomachs with water)...and see someone *home*.

Someone who appreciated, more than they could ever express, the chance for their brain to be stimulated in some approximation of the same ways that most people's were.

The senior partners read Morty's resume carefully when they hired him, and saw this aptitude, this empathy.

To the firm of Acosta, Blomberg and Black, placing the new blood there was simple asset-management. To Morty, it was Boot Camp 2.0 . He got over it. He got over everything. (No, really, he'd say. He did.)

But not this:

Someone from the firm had to come here once a month, stand his ground and put his hand out into the dark. Morty liked the idea of what he did there, and made himself expand the duties of the post so that the human touch was brought to it, beyond the drab scope of the client's wishes.

Just to show that they were earning their billable hours with Jim Heigner, the Vancouver aerospace tycoon better known around the offices of Acosta, Blomberg and Black as Daddy Warbucks, Morty was charged with engaging the "Posicore® Unit", the "decedent" (oh, there were times when the *lingua franca* of the *coerum al legis* drove him up down and sideways in relationship to the proverbial immovable wall,) in conversations of depth, to see that there was no decoherence, no decay, in any tiny qubit of the Posicore® brain woven into the cerebral cortex of the "decedent" like a ropy fungus gone fat on the flesh of a half-dead tree.

On a more human note, Morty was also teaching the girl Aikido. And chess. And knitting (though he promised the fleas of a thousand camels unto her if she ever told anyone he knew how to knit.) He streamed goofy music for her from his phonebead, into the parched suggestions of her shell-white ears: *Tom Lehrer pounding a barrelhouse piano and waxing rhapsodic about poisoning pigeons in the park, "The Three-Penny Opera"; Spike Jones and His City Slickers' "Moonlight Bay", something called a Weird Al Yankovic he found by mistake, and older songs a thousand times more obscure....*

It got to be a game with them. If Dolores couldn't find the song online, Morty won. If she could scour for it and got it, he had to bring in more...

In return, Dolores streamed homevid back into the phonebead, vid of a home so opulent Morty couldn't process it. Vid of a little girl with a shaved head, looking at herself in the mirror, the walking-sticks cinched on her arms clattering loudly in the silence.

Sometimes, he came other days than Wednesdays, bringing her things from her old room. Once, he couldn't, and he had to get Security to deliver the stuffed dragon.

He came to find sometimes that there was less in him than he ever knew, even after two hitches in Alaska. He'd seen guys lay on mines up there, and IED's, but this....

The little dead girl, his client's daughter, made a face at him and wiggled sickeningly up off the bed. Her clear gray visage always held a flat affect, though the eyes seemed to follow him. Morty's own face in the mirror when he got home on those Wednesday nights invariably resembled a full-head goblin mask.

Dolores was wearing a black hooded sweatshirt over gray pajamas. Bunny slippers. Wednesday outfit. This was always Wednesday, when he came for this part of it. Being in that room always unnerved him. He once knew a cancer patient whose house smelled like that. The guy lasted five years. Morty's neighbor. Eleven grand, it cost the super to fumigate...But it wasn't the smell, which was only mildly startling.

It was the curse of the expectation of the smell, when confronted with what your senses told you was clearly a corpse, a little music-box doll of a corpse that got up and walked around, and cracked jokes, but a corpse by any other name would be expected to smell like one.

Pausing, leaning on her sticks, Dolores Heigner fiddled with the oxygen plug where it was clipped to the septum of her small snub nose, doing something to the tube to make it stop occluding. Her tiny oval face glowed gray. She sat back down on the bed, a little closer to him, tracking him with the cameras behind her artificially-lubricated eyes.

Dolores' forehead gleamed dully in the stagnant fluorescent light as she turned to pantomime looking directly into his eyes with those huge, piercing China blues. The stapled coring scar above her left eyebrow looked like a question mark.

She was going to be a trillionaire. The parents kept the temporary flesh here in this private hospital bed, rotting in an attic like Rapunzel, the consciousness sealed off in the last augmentation she ever got, courtesy once more of Daddy Warbucks' minions who moistened the auggied flesh and kept the meds and vids fed.

Core-braining Dolores was the only way to cure the cancer. Cancer didn't grow in a dead body. They just had to keep her brain alive long enough for Daddy Warbucks to have a reliable new body grown from the collection of cells moving and breathing and whispering before him now.

Grown from a scraping of it, by off-Earth-human workers for a bowl of rice a day, on some asteroid that Morty couldn't even properly pronounce. What wouldn't they think of next?

Outside the window behind them, an airskiff went screaming grandiosely by. (It was a big lorry job hauling scrap metal, and dipped and swayed in the air ever-so-slightly.) "Where the hell are your parents in all this now?" Morty finally managed to ask.

"Same place they always were," Dolores whispered breathily, "Not here. I tried to talk to Mom about this. She put her fingers in her ears and called the Psych crew. She's... she never really adjusted well to anything, when you subtract those pills she takes on top of the vodka."

She could have been talking about a flick online. She pretended to sigh. "They'll grow me back and keep handing me off to Tesco," Daddy's mechassistant, "or Tessa," the artificial nanny, "Or... Anything but them. Anything but them."

At the sound of the repetition, Morty's head cocked. But her voice hadn't warbled the way it did when the brain got tired and the body needed to be recharged. This repetition was deliberate.

"Whether 'tis nobler in the mind to bear," he heard himself respond, "The slings and arrows of outrageous fortune, or to take arms against a sea of troubles, and by opposing, end them..."

Dolores's eyes held no affect at all. "Heard it. I have a lot of time to read. I've been a slave to money all my life, like, since I was born. You can't run from that. Can't ever live like regular people do."

Morty made a wordless noise of negation, hissing as though they'd both burned the same finger on a stove. Dolores plowed on regardless. If she'd been alive, she might have sounded petulant.

"I looked this up. I am an American citizen *and* a protected-class mecha. You're going to get me emancipated. Then I'm going to disconnect. And I'm going to die. Again. And there is nothing you can do about it."

"Whoa, whoa—" Morty held up his hands, but something in the girl's body language shooshed him. He was already thinking about a beer. And maybe hitting himself in the head with a hammer a few times. Because it would feel good when he stopped.

"They can't have me for their... breeding sow. I already saw the little monster from that other Multinational House that Daddy Warbucks... yes, I know what you call him at your office... wants to marry me off with when I get old enough for him to rut his nasty babies into me."

Those eyes swiveled toward him. "The creature is twenty-four. Presently. It has one eyebrow. It calls me 'pigeon.' I would not like to wake up to that. I will not. I am not. Morty, you can either help me, or you can go home."

Dolores got up again, leaning on her sticks. When she spoke, she'd pause occasionally and pace back and forth, trying to make the voder in her throat sync up somewhere near the speed of her thought process.

"I don't want to wind up like every other nasty teenaged harpy in my Dad's tax-caste, married to some tycoon's kid and whoring around with everything that can give them drugs. That's the worst place an American girl can sink, to have all the money in the world and no real parents, just a womb-donor and a sperm-donor who make you their sow."

Up pushed on Down pushed on Up. The world was spinning. Morty made himself listen.

"Even if I got out on my own, the damage has been done. I'd end up going to pieces with nothing to be mad at. I told you, I read up on this stuff. It's been like that in America for hundreds of years, and other girls think they should look *up* to us? Or make their own little play versions of *our* lives, and poison themselves the same way, for nothing? How screwed-up is that, Morty? Why wouldn't girls want to kill themselves before they're old enough to survive? We become..."

EE-EE-EE-EE... Dolores' eyes held the terror of a rabbit's last death-snarl in a taxidermist's front window. The voder couldn't continue. Air circulated into the boiling pouches of her lung-implants and wheezed a reflux up, up...

Morty couldn't blink. When she spoke again, Dolores Heigner's voice tolled like a temple gong. "EE-EE-EE..W..*We are all unsafe*. We are made into monsters. This world makes us into monster versions of ourselves. Like Daddy did to me, instead of letting me go. He can't let anything go that will make him money. "

Morty looked horrified. "Kid, no God-given life could be *that* terrible. You could get out somehow, get away, you... Aaah, forget about it. I can... I mean, I don't know from what I can *do* except listen, but..."

Something occurred to him. "Maybe that's why we get on so nice, you and me."

Swivel. He heard the whine of tiny, tiny optic motors. He plunged. "Nobody ever listened to you before. I'm an attorney, kid, I get paid to listen. You don't really want to die."

No sounds.

"Tell me about something you liked to do, before."

Dolores's former body nodded slowly, imperceptibly. "I used to sleep out in my treehouse, and watch the spaceships taking off at PDX," she informed him from left field, from a mouth and nose that didn't even breathe air any more. The air was close and stuffy in the room. The voder whirred like a furnace fan.

"Mike, the head Security guy at Dad's house, he had this puffy old Army sleeping bag he gave me to put out there. He said the spaceships looked like fireflies, that high up, and I had to get him to show me scans of what fireflies were. He showed me the moon, too, and the big mines in the Sea of Tranquility."

The sun and moon seemed to go round and round in that room. Morty closed his eyes, massaging his temples. Her voice rang in his ears. "You're a tough cookie," he heard himself say.

Dolores slithered towards him, using only basic muscle groups for motor movement. Morty knew there were silicon cables in there shoring up the ligaments, the bones, squittering beneath the skin. Some Assembly Had Been Required.

Wind echoed in the eaves of the tower. The air promised snow. The knee Morty barely brought back from Alaska was screaming just like he wanted to.

"Even when I'm switched all the way on, I keep seeing this white light. It makes it hard to see." She touched her temples. "And heat, here. And I hear voices singing in the wind outside. Calling me to come with them. "

Dolores jerked back over to him like a marionette and kissed him on the cheek. "You can go now, Mister Stein. Your energy level is down. Go get a burger. For me. With cheese on it, and onions, and ketchup and mayo and mustard."

Her eyes shone with tears, incredibly, and her lower lip shone with drool. "And all the French fries they have."

He had to leave when she told him to. Contractual obligation. At Sammy's Pub on the ground floor of the hospital, the cheeseburger went in a box with two bites out of it. Unfortunately, they didn't have take-out beers, so Morty had to pound a few. Which he did. And for that night, the last of many, he slept like a rock…

II

It was raining on the City of Roses, like this was news, raining on the haves and have-nots alike, the streets and the suites, the quick and the dead. It was raining for me and Jim. Not for Jim's little girl. For Dolores, it never rained, or snowed, or did anything.

I tweezed the phone in my earlobe and EAR VOLUME shot down three notches. Jim heard it. "Aaall… right, Stein. I know how I get with you FNG's. Duly noted. Let's go over this again."

FNG. That was Marine gunny-talk, drill-sergeant talk. It meant 'Fuckin' New Guy.' I wondered how long those three letters would show up on my forehead at the office, visible to everyone but me.

A world away, in my world, I stirred my coffee moodily and looked through two inches of space between the blinds. The phone squealed inside my ear. I tilted my head up and waited. The squeal went away.

"Mr. Heigner," I heard myself fire back. "Due respect, sir, you saw the vid from that room. I know why you called. Your little girl wants to die. I've already put 'Former Lawyer' on my Public Face online. Big deal. I wasn't going anywhere, anyway. Maybe I need to go shovel shit for a while, just to get the taste of that room out of my m---"

"Stein."

I waited again.

"Shut up. Let me think. What'd you say I pay you?"

I told him.

"Huh. Nominal. *Laughable.* You work for *me* now. No more firm. Come on out to the bunker. Senior partners"ll give you your golden handshake."

If I hadn't taken care of it some hours ago, I would have had a bowel void to write down on my own chart, and needed someone to change my diaper. "I..what...what..."

The floor went away, but I was still standing. I heard bugles in my ears, and the servo whine of bank terminals racheting out my four favorite words, PLEASE TAKE YOUR CASH. "Good." I could hear Heigner's teeth bare, when he chuckled. "You're flabbergasted. That means you're paying attention. Welcome to the family..."

III.

RECORDING: Test. Test. One-two. Test.

'But often, through the silent nights,
A funeral, with horns and lights
and music came to Camelot,
Or when the moon was overhead
Came two young lovers, lately wed.
'I am half-sick of shadows, said the Lady of Shallott...'

Okay, I got a level. I can hear the little recorder whining on the table, so I've kind of pointed my head toward it. Never tried this before.

Heigner's men took my eyes three years after I started. Three years was the shortest I ever held any job. They could have robbed me of far more painful bits. In that, they were merciful.

Dolores, just before I wake up in the morning, I dream that you're beside me, or out clattering around cooking something. Just before my eyes open all the way, in the false dawn whose pale, silvery effulgence is only powerful enough to light up the inner chambers of our hearts.

I can smell you on my skin, those mornings, feel you tugging at my heart from somewhere up there. Why do we never listen to what we know? I knew I was right the first time. I knew it was all futile.

I remember the first time I saw the new body they grew for you. That explained all the home-schooling, the doubling-up of information, the hypnopaedia and dataspikes and the whole nine.
    Coring and regrow aren't cheap. Daddy Warbucks probably didn't want to shell out for any more education than he had to.

He could afford it, but rich guys don't get rich by throwing money around. That just wasn't the way Jim thought.

They never told me the age, or the condition of your new body, the new mantle you now donned... or the way the light took your coppery hair when you turned your head to smile and ask Where Were We and I couldn't even operate my tongue.

What self-respecting girl *wouldn't* want that hard body, those eyes, the way your new face smiled like the Devil made you do it? I really never had any idea. Really. Never saw it coming.

I wish you'd answer my pings, from up there, where you are now. There's only one thing I ever want to know:

That you know, Dolores, that I'd never have given in, that first time, if you hadn't gotten up and closed the door behind us, and then come back over to sit beside me on the couch.

Your new body was doing the thinking. I wish I had that excuse. We both knew what would happen.

And we tried to break out anyway.

I knew I'd be disbarred, but the firm wasn't getting me anywhere. Remember that week we spent on Mars, in that mile-wide tourist hotel on Cydonia Reef? Remember? I suppose everything happened the only way it could, inevitably, inviolably, in a pig's ass. You're now one of the twenty richest humans on Earth. When you yell, people hit their knees.

I saw the CNN piece: You, just You, conducting that orchestra of holdings and assets and bottom lines by remote control, on floating panes of pure light, out in geosynchronous orbit where every hour is Dawn and not everything that moves can be identified.

They call you philanthropist now. I don't blame you for turning your back. Because your Dad made you watch what they did to me. And now you can't look at me.

And, kid, whether I want to or not, I sure as hell can't look at you.

But I understand. Once an attorney, always an attorney, kid. I understand too much.

Keep on funneling the assets of the Corporation Formerly Known As Heigner Aerospace right back to Earth, and the people in my city who need real jobs, and doctors for the bodies that are the only ones they ever get.

Hell, I'll have Heigner Eyes next year when they finish growing a match. Straight from a public-medical farm. You made that possible. That, and so much more. Keep up the Work. For me.

I understand how you seized your power, Dolores. I understand what happened, not long after you got home to Daddy Warbucks. Blind Justice down here dirtside can guess from that one fragmentary note you sent me. Especially the parts toward the end.

Rich girls know how to get what they want. But you knuckled down, instead... until you had to finally tell Daddy Warbucks off. When you couldn't take it any more.

He would have had a stroke, or a heart attack, if he was wound up enough. Those weird designer stimulants do it every time. Just needs a big enough reason to go Boom.

So you tweaked him. You let him have it. Hard enough that you knew he could either have a stroke or an embolism or a coronary...or be made to look like he did. I could never cast Stone One at you for that. You've got bigger stones than me, kid. Not the point.

But let's say he had his stroke. He had a headgear-plug in his left ear canal, from his eight years in the Corps. You had the old Posicore® unit that you told me they let you keep, in that note. The one you said 'met Daddy.' You plugged it in his left ear at the moment of truth, and the Thanatotic lock on military wetware did the rest. Now Safe To Remove Device. Ha. Ha.

*

Ha.

There is still earwax on the Posicore's tiny plug, earwax and blood and the faint lingering vibration of a long, cheated, petulant scream. I keep it in my top desk drawer. It still stinks like Daddy Warbucks.

I'm sorry, Morty. I think about you so much. One day, maybe we can heal. Until then, I've got my father right where I want him.

And I'm never, ever plugging him in.
Love always, D.H.

For Pat Cadigan and Larry Hall

Edward Morris is a 2011 nominee for the Pushcart Prize In Literature, also nominated for the 2009 Rhysling Award and the 2005 British Science Fiction Association Award. He has over a hundred short stories under his belt since 2002, most recently at Conjurings *("Yesterday Man" with Trent Zelazny,)* The Unwritten Review *and the* Lovecraft Ezine. *His novel* Blackguard 2: The Art of War *just went to press at Wildside Books, and his breakout series* A Crooked Man *(covers by Nick Gucker, edits by Joseph Pulver)will be out soon from Mercury Retrograde Press.*

35

JOIN THE CLUB
by Hal Duncan

I had to shave my head to join the club. Village culture can be like that, even when the village is actually a neighbourhood within a city. It wasn't explicit. I wasn't refused entry by the shaven-headed men in their shiny black bomber jackets. I was served at the bar... eventually. Nobody took me aside and asked me to leave. But it was made very clear, in their eyes. Yes, physically I was *in the club*, but I didn't really *belong*, not with that haircut. I had to take the razor, shave my skull to suede or smooth skin.

I had to get a tattoo to join the club. The first few nights I went— Saturday this week, Friday the next—it was just a matter of paying on the door, getting an X in black ink on the back of your hand. So you could go outside for a smoke, you know, and get back in. Then they began to use a little stamp, something not unlike an X, but a little more intricate, less easily copied. Then they brought in one of those library book date-stamps. The tattoo was just easier, they said eventually. Permanent membership.

I had to wear a badge to join the club. Everyone was wearing the badge, the same way everyone was wearing their heads shaved, the same way everyone was wearing those shiny black bomber jackets with tartan lining, and the tight jeans, and the shiny black boots. These were all markers of identity, of pride in oneself—a fierce defiant pride. Because no matter what anyone said, we had the right to be what we were, and together we could stand up to Them. The badge declared our Truth. Was it a pink triangle or a Union Jack? You decide.

I had to march with a flag to join the club. There were those who hated Us, those who had to be shown that their conspiracies against Us would not win. They had infiltrated all corners of society, the media and the government. They were spreading lies about Us, plotting our deaths in fire. We had to march down the streets where They lived, past the corner-shops where They might well work, selling the newspapers that were little better than propaganda. We had to chant in unison to show Them that we were an army. Organised, resolute, unafraid. Rising.

I had to board a train to join the club. That was where the march ended up: at the train station. One club, one village, one city wasn't enough. We had to spread out across the land. We had to gather in camps in distant places inaccessible to most, places where we would be safe, with our own kind. I had to follow the others onto the train. I had to lead them, drive them on. It wasn't a time for doubts, for questions. Questions were to be met with torture, murder. We had no choice. We had no choice.

    door.

Hal Duncan *is a Scottish science fiction and fantasy writer. whose books include* Velum, Ink *and* Escape From Hell.

LADYBUG DAY
by Cameron Pierce

The blue sky was choked with screaming white.

Then a cloud crawled by on darkened tortoise limbs.

The first rain of August.

A century of carcinogenic waste churning along the bottom.

A liquid jungle made of shit.

The rain pitter-pattered against a red tent beneath the bridge.

Bob drained the last acrid gulp of a warm forty.

He dropped his cigarette butt into the glass bottle.

He scratched at his bruised, liver-spotted face.

He climbed out of the soiled tent, carrying a fishing pole in one hand and a tin cigarillo case in the other.

The case was filled with lead weights, hooks, and bugs, mostly alive.

Grasshoppers, spiders, worms, ladybugs, and crickets lived together in the case.

A fisherman had to keep an assortment.

Bob was a good fisherman.

Bob kept it fresh.

What caught twenty bass one day might catch none the next.

Bob squinted at the rain-pocked river and nodded.

"Today'll be ladybugs, I bet," he said, and then he called back to the tent. "Buddy, get up."

Buddy spilled out of the tent and landed on all fours, vomiting.

"Shut yer asshole," Buddy said, getting to his feet.

Bob tied on a treble hook and pinched on two egg-shaped sinkers and opened the tin case, first giving it a gentle shake to stun the bugs.

He chose a ladybug at a time.

Three ladybugs total.

He slid a rusted spear into their dark bellies and through their bright-black shells.

The ladybugs squirmed.

They looked like flames flecked with ash.

Bob smiled at the pretty ladybugs.

He would have a bass on in no time.

Buddy came to stand beside Bob.

Vomit on his shoes and shirt.

Buddy carried his own pole and tackle box.

Buddy's tackle box was a tin Buck Rodgers lunchbox.

Both of them believed that tin boxes of any kind preserved bait better, but they never spoke about it.

"What's we havin' today?" Buddy said.

"Ladybugs," Bob said, and he cast out toward some decayed pilings in the river.

"Seems mo like 'asshoppas myself," Buddy said.

"Hell, go with grasshoppers," Bob said.

"Think I will," Buddy said.

"Whatever works," Bob said.

Bob's sinkers hit bottom and he flipped the bail.

Bass frequently nested at the base of those pilings.

Once you discovered a spawning bed, you could catch bass in your sleep.

Buddy baited up with a fat grasshopper.

He walked a couple dozen yards along the rocky bank.

He cast out upriver from Bob.

The rain soaked through their clothes but it was a warm day.

Bob's ladybugs claimed the first bass.

The fish hit close to shore.

Buddy cranked in his line and hurried over to see.

Bob fought the bass in the rest of the way and held the fish up by the gills for Buddy.

"Thas a pig," Buddy said.

"Told you, iz ladybugs," Bob said.

He slit the fish's gills with a rusted knife to bleed it out.

He slid the bass onto the long copper wire that he used for a stringer, and then he tied the stringer around a steel pole that had been pounded into the earth.

"Think I'm sticking with these 'asshoppas fo a little bit mo," Buddy said.

"So you stickin' with grasshoppers then."

"Feels like 'asshoppas today."

"Remember it ain't what you like, it's what the fishes like," Bob said, baiting up with three more ladybugs from his cigarillo case.

"True dat," Buddy said, and he returned to his spot upriver.

They fished for a while longer without much happening.

The rain fell harder.

Bob freshened his ladybugs at some point.

Buddy vomited several times.

It could have been that he was hung over, but he was always hung over.

The scared animal look in his eyes suggested that something else was the matter.

There was a pleading look behind his bloodshot irises that begged *Please, let nothin' be wrong.*

Bob caught another bass, then another.

They would eat bass for dinner that night, as they had done every night before and would continue to do every night thereafter.

"Told you iz a ladybug day," Bob said.

Buddy tried to speak, but the pain in his gut was too great.

All Buddy could do was smile as the rain poured down and Bob caught bass after bass on ladybugs until the sun went down and they lit a fire beneath the bridge and cooked the bass and ate the bass and crawled into the tent and got fucked up on the last of their supply and lay shivering side by side in the dark and finally Buddy felt better but still he could not speak and the pain was growing, swelling upward into his chest, and every so often Bob opened his cigarillo case and talked to his bugs, maybe stroking one, and one of these times a grasshopper escaped.

Right then is when it happened, faster than expected, like the sun bursting out in the middle of a rainstorm.

Even in the dark, Bob must have sensed it.

He forgot all about his grasshopper.

He put a hand on Buddy's chest.

He said, "Buddy, you okay?"

Cameron Pierce is the Wonderland Book Award-winning author of eight books, most recently Die You Doughnut Bastards. *He is also the head editor of Lazy Fascist Press and has edited three anthologies, including* The Best Bizarro Fiction of the Decade. *He lives in Portland, Oregon with his wife, author Kirsten Alene*

Chris Shaw

GOOD FRIDAY
by Dave Migman

we will dine upon each others throats
milk white and honey drool
thrash it out till the remnants
of the moon
shiver over this haunted city
of mists

we will fuck each other into
the early hours and I
shall be conscious
of my early rising
the profanity of hours
and eyes, the hollow
empty pit when the street cops
turn their attentions my way
tell me to pack and
leave

but tonight I will gobble
you up and you will
use your sex toys on me
I will submit
until the dusky blue
coughs enchanting haikus
from the lips
of lost revelers still stoned
through morning.

IN THE WAKE OF YOUR CERTAINTY
by Dave Migman

I do not pretend to understand the wind
how it moves me, how I am surrendered,
sundered, betrayed, vilified, exulted to rise,
collected regrets cast away, the expectations
of every little sigh, your flighty laughter
the porous minds of brothers and sisters
the deluge contained in each raindrop.

the essence shifts, contextual chameleons:
truth is in essence an unobtainable hunger
in our foolish breasts, filling our thoughts,
our books are blemished with truth, as though
to expel the idea and bind it to
the page deems it 'true'

do not pretend to know the rain
or the dust that glitters on the moon
or the flowers bursting through skulls
or the way, when his last breath left
the old man was a husk cast in cold mud,
jaundiced, lifeless and empty
and the birds still sang outside the window
and the grey skies still pour within with you!

THE HALLOWED DIRT
by Dave Migman

I cannot concede this
negative influence; my prerogative
to negotiate false dawns and idols
your idleness – these things
crowd in with driving nails
rain down to crush my creosote
hide, my pride – my pride
my shotgun pride, the vision
of youth, like predilections of
the warrior blood gene that
cannot back down or join in
or adore your enforced good time
or the way you police
your happy thoughts, your happy
time, while ¾ of the world
starves or fights, you point
at me and shake your dreadlocked
guru-self-satisfied-middle-class
-hippy-bastard-scum-fuck-heads and tuck me back
into the dirt

Dave Migman *is an artist, on-air talent and the author of* The Wolf
Stepped Out.

AND THE BASS KEEPS THUMPIN'
by Joseph S. Pulver, Sr.

In one of my fiery moods (they don't vaccinate for aggression where I'm from). Stopped in the Sea Horse Tavern to pay Nicky and Buk for Tuesday's run. Didn't hang. Wanted some pussy and sure as 12cold-fucks, Mabel (who filmed a few of Tralala 600s back in the day) ain't a menu item.

Split.

Urged for seXwinkin' (tits'n'ass, hold the swastikas and petulantly) Lolitas whose saliva and syllables would *yes*;Gladly. Knew the spot where all the edges are avant and enthusiastic.

Crosstown. Lower. No one checks the clock, they check the drums. Rents don't get paid. "*. . . todas las cosas que no volveremos a existir.*"

No weather to speak of…

Devil's in my rearview. Can't say the hair looks all that stylish… but the horns I sport are real fine.

Rolled by jazz—wasn't upholstered by Lester Young, barely turned my head… slid by heroin…

Neon-herbs crimpin' the risk in the frame… No triggers with a fistful of bullets (So far. Tonight.)

Caddy up on blocks.

bent with a few corners…

Pontiac Pizza… Side2 Wings & Sushi… The Neutral (that sure as shit ain't!)…

SALEM **MARLBORO** BEER **LOTTO** *BEER*

rats…

Wildflower Washing Machine…

ain't newyork but the pattern's the same—lie; lure; aggressively; alley with never-stopping in the back; spit; needles; unable; rapist; slut;

FUCK YOU—

rats didn't pause from their garbage conventions to note my passing… never do…

Predator's side of town: corner of Galaxy and North Hazelwood. Pack 'em in tittie-joint called Guerlain's *NEON BONEYARD*…

The male-hustlin' endeavors of a bottle-blonde sportin' twin-44s lovin' her salty trip with the pole. Confetti snows, she fluttered, the Jacksons fluttered rarin'-to-go replies… banshees… landfill mouths… molecular hallucinating therapy for their scars… injuries wedged in between Narcissistic and specializing-in-S-&-M… drunk, Xanax, coke, sugar and spice…

lot of pussy.

lots of dreamin' dicks that will never touch it. they'll go home to a can of soup and softporn zilla-tits on cable.

All GRRRRRRRRRRRL house-band. *Nice Lipstick.* Twin guitars—both blondes, both punk Barbies, both damn good players, Vox organ instigating a rave-up (you gotta love the Northwest, 50years after and she's crowned with a Paul Revere and the Raiders Revolutionary War tricorne), coaxing drums (bass drum says Booty, and comes'ta funk she's got it all up in her stuff)…

Electric chair cannibal-bass is thumpin'—

HER bass.

Ass (that puts voltage in my revolution!) wigglin' like that—offerin' a man a meal, and me, I'm always hungry—Plate it up!

Two punk-assbags boppin' next to me say her name is, Nikki, say it like some prayer that leads your ambition from exile to the blossom of Paradise.

"Nikki." I like its taste on my tongue. "Nikki." I'd be happy to assault her (crannies & FELT) with a downpour of graphic detail.

I'm locked on her 6.

Want it!

BAD!

I know she is. Will be.

Wants to be!

I see it—her BLAST, her new breed, uncompromising, baking her savage, building her adrenaline masterpieces to purest.

Wants my de Sade rippin'—arched back squirrelin' body molds and 'ploitation! Ebb&flow in every aeon of her FELT—

48

Living doll GRRRRRRL power—jump-outta-her-shoes, nakedfleshkarma-FRENZY of slobberin'/grunting/shovin' her ass to juicy-expelled, to raise her broken angel.

Gonna!

Back the bottle. Need its cold.

Back to the viewin'… Fishnets (I like the hole in 'em behind her right knee), green skirt up to her *de raw*, spaghetti straps on a Hello Kitty as the Bride of Frankenstein tee… TOP ta BOTTOM & INMOST I'm runnin' hot.

LUST—the teeth of me/myself/'n'/I! GLUTTONY! GREED! LUST! LUST! lust

And her bass keeps thumpin'…

And my bottle is empty.

Flamed-fueled UP & READY, volcano and hurricane runnin' with my Old Devil and that STRUTTIN'ass with that no-hidin'-it shuffle, there's an INFERNO in my crypt.

Set's over. I catch her at the bar. Scheherazade-*Chanel* teasing me, offering me kingdom come, smile offerin' a variant spelling. Front's even better than the *sa-weet*back, not a shy river in her. Blue eyes… and that mole. Incident of INFERNOred hair got my skip-along skippin'—leapin' too, brow and pale of her neck glistening. Nothing like a beastess-in-heat sweatin' fer ya. Tats and tits—Cherries fer the RIPE of me! She's got my pinpoint, PSYCHO, and dependant, pegged-11 and DEADRED on *acquisition*.

Says, "I love your "Give me *Philosophy in the Boudoir*, or I give you DEATH" tee. Smiles, obscenely version.

Should I, beg? Sweetly? Sleazy? All sezy-like? The devil canal in me just wants to grab and start inhaling. BUT—

The 2 longnecks I'd ordered to cool me arrive, I slide her one. Wait . . . If she picks it up I'm gonna scratch her name in my diary, highlight it with the words *sexual MISSadventure*, mouth, hair, SCREAM that made Joyce Mansour blush.

"Thanks." Quick bottle back, 3rd of it. "Sometimes you *need*. If you know what I mean?"

Did she just wink?

Must have, as I saw it.

"Nights you just want someone to steal your cascade . . ." Laughs, her sezy soaks me. "My wounded lunatic gets seized and the constellation in my temple needs here it comes."

49

Nikki drains half the bottle. Draining is an activity I would never think to restrict… or thwart.

"You have any needs?"

"They're all on the map in my car. The car that wanted to be parked in my driveway 3 seconds after I saw you shakin' all over."

"Let's go and fuck." Plain as I'd put it if I was bold.

"Your chariot waits."

"I was hoping for a *muscle* car." Intoxicating mouth. "Seems I have affections of libidinous VAROOM-VAROOM in mind." Slither/snap/pop soft wet lips that won't wait to give me my birthday gift.

"At'sa me. Horsepower. You be nice and I'll show you where the HD in my HP tops out."

"You promise to be merciless?"

"Didn't I mention my name is, Ming?"

"I was sure you were going to say, de Sade. I'm really a *Juliette* by the way, but I use Nikki. It's oh so sezy."

As the yes you can't say no to. As the waters of March, as the relaxed-fit moon opening here it is.

Sezy mouth open, not a word dislodged, I nodded my IS.

She's hot to GO/I've rarely been keener.

FAST EXIT:

24 hour butcher shop called The Ethical Butcher.

"Bloody steak and a meaty fuck. That's what I go for," she says. "Maybe pick up some meat for later?"

We do.

Best they have.

Gentleman that I am I let her pick the cut.

And we're rollin'—

Out passed the Dead Swamp (such pretty appointments, most souvenirs that were gifts from me), passed the crossroads to LandsEND where the *BABYLON DELIRIO MOTEL* flickers its VAC NCY and just a might more sits my abode… Made it to my lion's den in 15flat. NEED (a shape-shifting swell of dazzle confirmed) and WANTsssssS and the prettiest, skin-tight little ass this side of I WANNA BE YER DOG, BABY will do that.

Polite (hopin' to earn pussy-points) would have offered her the Grand Tour. Mama didn't try to fit me with politician and urbane.

Scent of earthquakes-triggered on us, took about 3eyeblinks to get inside—less to get to unwrapped—

prettiest 34D tits and sweat.andsweet ass and beer{in her bellybutton and cleavage} and hot doggies and we're a 2-hysteria daisychain—ankles(seems like they're flying around the room like an hungry shark) and wetlands-cunt{wantin' what it wants!} dealin' hope, and palms roaring. and her tits smotherin' my what's for dessert.got a cherry tat in my mouth and her nipple is screamin' for its due. 5feet5 of squirrely-rollercoaster that's takin' the shaft—yank&yank and squeezin' the ironsides to ooze and burst{with extra KACHANG}, no jive.

And I haven't even got her panties off yet.

Nor have we had our appetizer.

It's still hanging there all ripe and pretty. Trussed up soNICENICE in ballgag and cuffs, party balloons heaving. It's looking at me like I'm an oncoming bulldozer, or 666 . . . *Close.* I toss it a wink and a grin. Add a blown kiss. I like to think its steeping. Groom it right and it tastes better.

Hungry we— Fang—my tattoo Draculass nips me, drop for drop I give good as I get, rod wicked for encore, slice o warmdelight expressin' again-dialogue, and, of course, OURvigorous. After we got that 1st kiss out of the way, lube up and set the controls for the heart of the INFERNO.

Yeah. Let din-din simmer some…

So it's back to the reverie-waltz -adjoined -renderin' -blurred -every inch -labia -hug -slippery -thrust -good pussy (open sticky as figs) -great nectar pussy of raw wet miracles —fistfuls yielding – wobble—pinch/slap/KISS –spin/singe –no pussyfooting –milelong tongues as soft as black calla lilies in crazy moonlight -beautiful face -beautiful clit -bull's eye "Fuck me. FUCK me. Fuck… that's goo*ooooooo*od. God…" **"Again!"**

"Damn, baby."

And just when I'm ready for stars and the last ZOOM & Finale of this auto-de-YAY my Juliette is up and outta bed. Prancin' 'round.

Tits bouncing. Shakin' that sweetass for (and AT) me.

I give up another "WOW". Nikki's got the motor-booty thumpasorusBUMP goin' down. 'nother 'round o ME-*weeeeeeeeeeeeeee* gots'ta have (and hold on sinTIGHT).

SHAKE!
Me. IT!
SHAKE!
shake-shake-that nova-maker! !!
"Like that, Daddy?"
My head bobbin' DO—*Gimme!*
LIGHTNING—

Snapped her tang into a pinup pose, noted I was ready to FRY. Blew me a succupuss kiss. "And you haven't even seen what I can do with my tail."

"Tail?"

"Was saving my little *surprise* for you." Winks. Offers my heart the fizz of a chuckle. Blows me a kiss—I'm nuked. "Hope you like."

And out it comes. My celebrate of fascinated is changed right down to my neurons, my tongue takes on new energies. Nikki has a tribal, dragon tramp stamp on slow curve of her lower back and where the tail ends at the top of her backfield-cleavage 3slender-feet of fine soft, (barber-pole striped) red fur—red as her hyperthyroidNEON locks, has come out to play. Never seen a kittycat with a tail that fine—Never... My mood ring eyes aglow as it snakes out and rings the full-throated Thereness of my *helloooo* kitty...

The first stroke is *piece de resistance* s_ _l_o_ _ _w_
and soft
{strokin' a kittycat s~o~f~t}

—I'm chittering, and may have let out a WOW (in fact I'm sure of it)—

—she's feeding me her cherries—

DON'T THINK THE SOFT WILL LAST LONG

Nikki slides a 4.125" *Buck Zipper* out of the sheath lashed to the side of her boot. It's a conductor's baton in her slender fingers. "And when I'm done milking this cunt-loving rod . . . It's time for our bloody steak."

Our appetizer's eyes scream what the ball gag prohibits...
is.

.

52

Joseph S. Pulver, Sr. *is the author of the novels* The Orphan Palace *(Chomu Press 2010) and* Nightmare's Disciple *(Chaosium 1999), and he has written many short stories that have appeared in magazines and anthologies, including* Weird Fiction Review, Crypt of Cthulhu, *and* Lovecraft eZine, *Ellen Datlow's* Best Horror of the Year, *S. T. Joshi's* Black Wings *(I and III; PS Publishing) and* A Mountain Walked *(Centipede Press 2013), Ross Lockhart's* Book of Cthulhu *(Night Shade 2011), and many anthologies edited by Robert M. Price. His highly-acclaimed short story collections,* Blood Will Have Its Season, SIN & ashes, *and* Portraits of Ruin, *were published by Hippocampus Press in 2009, 2010, and 2012, respectively.*

He edited A Season in Carcosa *and* The Grimscribe's Puppets *(Miskatonic River Press 2012 and 2013), and collections by Ann K. Schwader (*The Worms Remember*) and John B. Ford, and Edward Morris'* A Crooked Man *series (Mercury Retrograde Press 2013).*

His new collection, Stained Translations, *edited by Jeffrey Thomas, will appear in 2013 from Dark Regions Press.*

GREAT HORROR AT 40% OFF
Find a selection of Imperial Youth in the sublime horror anthology, *Terror Scribes.*

Scan the QR code for your discount, or visit lulu.com/spotlight/doghorn.

Terror Scribes is a satisfyingly diverse anthology, furnished with nebulous, original tales guaranteed to set your teeth on edge and give you bouts of gooseflesh. From the home-grown talent of Sue Phillips to prolific US gore-hound Deb Hoag, from the satirists to the psychopaths to the traditionalists, from demonic possession of celebrities to masturbating werewolves, from hair-raising fairytales to disturbing accounts of everyday terror, you will shiver and gasp and question. We are not oblivious to the fear Terror Scribes will evoke. Quite the contrary, we're advocates of it . . .

A Visit to Dad the Comic

excerpted from *Vital Fluid*
a feature-length screenplay
by Tom Bradley

EXT. "OFF-OFF-STRIP" NIGHTCLUB—NIGHT

Situated at the edge of an interstate off-ramp in the middle of the Nevada wasteland, the "Off-Off Strip" is the end of the line for failed Las Vegas acts.

The marquee reads—

PROFESSOR PERCIVAL and SHIT-HEEL the DUMMY!

An endless stream of eighteen-wheelers screams by, abusing their klaxon horns, toying deliberately with Doppler effect to annoy the few patrons of this night club.

INT. "OFF-OFF-STRIP" DRESSING ROOM

In the mirror, surrounded by light bulbs, about half of which need changing, a decrepit face looks at itself with self-loathing and terminal hopelessness.

PROFESSOR PERCIVAL is the unlucky owner of this face. He's dressed in a baggy old academic gown, black. On the makeup table at his elbow, next to a bottle of cheap whiskey, is a black mortarboard-type graduation cap with a frayed brown tassel.

A ventriloquist's dummy, namely SHIT-HEEL, lies in a box on the floor. He's a college freshman, complete with a letter sweater and a dunce-cap, which has been stapled to his head at a pugnacious angle.

Via the mirror, Professor Percival sees blurred motion behind his shoulder. Then the new arrival comes into focus. It's his son, PHIL, a professional stage hypnotist, come for a rare visit.

Phil is dressed in an electric-blue tux with a plum satin cummerbund. His hair is done in the big way of professional stage entertainers, and his face is made up in a theatrical way.

PROFESSOR PERCIVAL
My son, The New Svengali. I don't suppose
you can hypnotize the 'cock-sucking manager
to turn off the boob tube over the bar.

PHIL
Are you kidding? On the night of the big game?

PROFESSOR PERCIVAL
What big game?

PHIL
How should I know?

PROFESSOR PERCIVAL
It's bad enough for me, but for you TV's
a thorough ass-fuck. They're already a mile
under before you come on.

PHIL
If only the power would go off. A statewide
blackout. We could work wonders by candlelight.

PROFESSOR PERCIVAL
Wonder-working's your gig. I just piss people
off. Or try to. If they ignore me again tonight,
I'm fixing to do my patented Christ Climax.

PHIL
Well, like they say, red makes green. No, wait,
that's the World Wrestling Federation.

Professor Percival sucks on his cheap whiskey.

PHIL
Come on, now, Dad. Don't you remember what that
stuff tastes like?

Phil makes the hand gesture that he uses to put his subjects under
hypnosis.

PROFESSOR PERCIVAL
Sure. Mmmm. Delicious.

Even as the professor gulps, Shit-Heel's voice emanates from the box
on the floor.

SHIT-HEEL
You should never have told him it was unleaded.

Phil looks unhappy as his old man takes yet another swig.

PROFESSOR PERCIVAL
Don't worry, sonny-boy. You're a good healer.

SHIT-HEEL
(from the box)
Certain filthy old lushes are just incurable.

INT. "OFF-OFF-STRIP" NIGHTCLUB—A BIT LATER

Professor Percival and Shit-Heel the Dummy are doing their routine.
The latter is on the lap of the former, whose ass is on a spot-lit folding
chair up front.

Phil watches from the bar, wincing already.

The bleached old BAR MAID brings him a beer.

BAR MAID
Your daddy's just the cutest little old thing.
Shit-Heel, maybe not so much.

A moderate earth-temblor rattles the bottles behind the bar and
clinks the ice everyone's cocktails. Not that anybody notices—the
television above the bar is on.

Nevertheless, as if the temblor is his cue, Shit-Heel goes into a panic.

SHIT-HEEL
We'll all be killed!

He buries his head, dunce-cap and all, in Professor Percival's gown.

SHIT-HEEL
(voice muffled)
You can really feel those H-bomb tests way
out here in the middle of Butt-Fuck Egypt.

PROFESSOR PERCIVAL
(a kindly, if pedantic, old gentleman)
This is technically still the Las Vegas Strip,
you know. I-15 is a continuation of—

SHIT-HEEL
(sticking his head out)
Shut the fuck up, geezer.
(sticking his head back in)

PROFESSOR PERCIVAL
(apparently hard of hearing)
In downtown, Las Vegas, the nuclear bomb tests
often tend to be far less noticeable, what with
all the asphalt holding things together.

A big fart puffs out the professor's gown. Shit-Heel scrambles out, reeling.

                    SHIT-HEEL
          You could use something to hold the fault in
          your ass together.

So far, nobody in the audience has acknowledged the dummy's existence, much less the professor's.

Even the Bar Maid looks as though she's reconsidering her opinion of Phil's daddy's cuteness.

Another nuke goes off, and the dummy dives for cover again. This time he comes up with a giant boner pushing up the front of his pants like a tent-pole.

                    SHIT-HEEL
          Sorry, everybody, heh heh. Power excites me.

                    PROFESSOR PERCIVAL
          It's the ultimate aphrodisiac, as Dr. Henry
          Kissinger once remarked to Chairman Mao Ze—

                    SHIT-HEEL
              (screaming, with sincere hate)
          Didn't I tell you to shut the fuck up? Why don't
          you just die, old man?

Professor Percival ponders Shit-Heel's suggestion. Then he pauses a bit longer to survey the unresponsive audience.

                    PROFESSOR PERCIVAL
          Okay.

He has opted for the Christ Climax.

Professor Percival gets up and turns the dummy loose on the biggest, drunkest BRUISER in the room, hoping the guy will kill them both.

                    SHIT-HEEL
        Come on, fudge-packer. Pay attention. Grampy
        wants you to get miffed and rise up and beat
        him to death. You know, suicide by mongoloid.

The Bruiser hardly notices. Neither does his aging GIRLFRIEND,
who is seated next to him.

                    SHIT-HEEL
        All right, lard-ass. Just sit there.
                (to Girlfriend)
        Madam—and I use the term lightly—would you
        happen to have a loaded Glock concealed between
        those rolls of gut, or breasts, or whatever you
        want to call them? Let me check.

Shit-Heel commences groping her.

She just flicks his little wooden hand off, not even looking away
from the television, which is showing an ad for an enormous SUV.

It's cool silvery-blue vehicle, and seems to float in slow motion
through the Earth's most beautiful scenery. The vehicle itself has
been photographed so skillfully as to make you hardly notice its
gorgeous surroundings.

The music is intoxicating, and the girl behind the wheel has hair like
liquid sunshine and a really nice rack.

Even videophobic Phil's looking.

Shit-Heel won't stop groping the Girlfriend. He gets another boner,
a really big one this time—modestly clothed, like the previous one,
in his trousers.

                    SHIT-HEEL
        Sorry. Decrepit trailer trash excites   me, too.
        I'm sick that way.

He waves it in their faces.

> BRUISER
> (absently)
> Yeah. Nice. Real good. Thanks.

Without thinking or removing his eyes from the screen, he brushes Shit-Heel's boner aside.

The Girlfriend doesn't even do that. She just cranes her neck around it.

> BRUISER
> Those are some sweet wheels.

> GIRLFRIEND
> Really.

The life leaves the professor's eyes, once and for all. Relaxing his dummy arm, he walks silently off, dragging Shit-Heel like the chunk of dead wood he is.

INT. PHIL'S CAR—WEE HOURS

Phil is driving his dad home.

Professor Percival sits in the death seat, withering into himself with despair till he looks no bigger than Shit-Heel, who remains parasitically fastened onto his lap, hissing Chopin's Funeral March into his ear with great cruelty.

EXT. RUN-DOWN LAS VEGAS NEIGHBORHOOD—DAWN

It's a zone of vacant lots and abandoned cars. The whole block on the verge of being reclaimed by the desert.

Phil's car passes the STAR DUST TALENT AGENCY, located in a shabby office on top of a garage.

SHIT-HEEL (VO)
Are you going to drop in on our so-called
agent while you're in town?
PHIL (VO)
Why? Just in case he's found some rich and
powerful movers and shakers who want to be
hypnotized? I doubt Mo's got a time machine in there.

The car pulls into a raunchy trailer park.

INT. PROFESSOR PERCIVAL'S TRAILER—A FEW MOMENTS
LATER

Phil is trying to tuck the professor in bed, academic gown and all,
but the dummy is reluctant to leave his lap. Shit Heel seems to sense
that it might be the last time he gets to straddle and torment the old
man.

As Phil tries to pull him off, Shit Heel looks askance at Phil's stage
hypnotist drag, hair and makeup.

SHIT-HEEL
(with a camp lisp)
Looks like a certain somebody has come out
since we saw her last. I hope you haven't brought
AIDS into our home, you slut.

When Phil finally manages to wrench him loose, Shit-Heel yelps like
a patient at the climax of a proctology examination.

SHIT-HEEL
Yow! Just 'cause Dad always liked me best!

Phil holds the obnoxious chunk of wood at arm's length, and tries to
ignore its chatter.

PHIL
I've always wondered if it's the college-boy
son you never had.

PROFESSOR PERCIVAL
(gasping from his pillow)
Fuck college. It just would've been nice to have
a son who followed in my footsteps.

There's an uncomfortable silence, during which Phil and his dad both gaze at Shit-Heel, the professor wistfully, Phil with a hint of sibling rivalry.

Shit-Heel, finding himself surrounded, shakes his head, as if to say, "What a couple of matched assholes."

Professor Percival chooses this moment to breathe his last. While cruel snickers emanate from the dummy in Phil's hands, the old man commences his death rattle, hideously loud.

SHIT HEEL
(to Phil, over the death rattle)
Way to go. You broke his poor old heart. How
hard would it have been to invest in a dummy
and learn to throw your voice? Just a couple feet?
You as good as killed him. And another thing—

Shit-Heel goes on and on.

But Phil's not listening because, through the frayed rayon curtains, he has caught a glimpse of a TV in the trailer next door. There's a skinny, huge-mouthed, husky-voiced woman on it, and she talks earnestly about something or other.

Taking a seat on the edge of his father's death-bed, holding a yammering Shit-Heel on his knee, Phil, the World's Greatest Stage Hypnotist, digs in for a few hours of voyeuristic television.

INT. PROFESSOR PERCIVAL'S TRAILER—NEXT MORNING

Phil's heading out the door, looking a little confused.

Shit-Heel's been chattering nonstop the whole time.

> SHIT HEEL (OS)
> (from under the bed,
> where Phil has stuffed him)
> —and thanks, by the way, for finishing Dad off.
> I was getting sick of him. Now let's go dig up
> several casual sex partners. There's a lumberyard
> just up the road, if you take my meaning, and—

Tom Bradley is the author, most recently, of Three Screenplays *(Dog Horn Publishing),* Family Romance *(Jaded Ibis Press) and* Felicia's Nose *(MadHat Press), both illustrated by Imperial Youth Artist Nick Patterson. Lately he has published* A Pleasure Jaunt With One of the Sex Workers Who Don't Exist in the People's Republic of China *(Neopoiesis Press),* Even the Dog Won't Touch Me *(Ahadada Press),* Hemorrhaging Slave of an Obese Eunuch *(Dog Horn Publishing),* My Hands Were Clean *(Unlikely Books) and* Put It Down in a Book *(The Drill Press), which was named* 3:AM Magazine's *Non-Fiction Book of the Year 2009. Tom's next two books are collaborations with Imperial Youth artist David Aronson:* We'll See Who Seduces Whom: a graphic ekphrasis in verse *will be launched at &Now 2013 by Unlikely Books; and a graphic novel, with secret title and hidden nature, is on the way from the occultural publisher, Mandrake of Oxford. Further curiosity can be indulged at tombradley.org.*

CLAIM 40% OFF THE RETAIL PRICE
Scan the QR code with your smartphone's barcode reader app to check out Tom's latest book, *Three Screenplays* or visit lulu.com/spotlight/doghorn.

RRP: £12.99. Offer price: £7.79.

VODOU
by Joseph Robicheaux

On all occult subjects, there are many trivial arguments in which one may discuss all points of regarding what is most pure, or most like the original. These have been exhausted, and there is nothing more to say. In this era were every Tom, Dick, and Harry is a consummate internet debater, and expert, some topics can become quite heated when they do not require the attention (or tension) they are creating for themselves and others. However most modern people are not often willing or able to admit that we enjoy participating in or reading the threads created by two arguing parties on the internet. So here I present one of my favorite arguments in my sphere of interest. New Orleans Voodoo: does it exist? Or is it all Hoodoo? And if new Orleans Voodoo is not real because of is mixing of ideas, Is Haitian Voodoo considered real? And if by following the string of ideas would that make the only real Voodoo from Benin? As a practitioner and devout believer in Voudou, I consider all the points, that I will attempt in brief to discuss with out any partisan, for me being pro one opinion versus the other, perhaps this is because I believe all of these traditions are all valid in their own ways.

To briefly discuss the topic of the ADR (African Diaspora Religions) Voudou, Voodoo, Vadou and all of its other spellings is perhaps the most recognizable of all of the faiths, Voodoo is a monotheistic religion with a cavalcade of terrestrial and celestial spirits, whose origins are in animism. The center of the belief of Voodoo is in West Africa in the areas of Nigeria, Ghana and central Benin. This area along with the Congo, was the epicenter of the triangular slave trade. The slaves brought with them their music, cultures and religions, and one of the many faiths they brought with them was Voodoo, the western center of this religion is the Caribbean island of Haiti, then in antiquity called Hispaniola. In Haiti's own history a revolution fueled by their belief in Voodoo helped the only successful slave rebellion come in to existence, which then allowed Mean while in North America in the Louisiana purchase in the city of New Orleans, the slave population is almost entirely Congolese and Angolan. While they had their own indigenous beliefs they also had knowledge of Voodoo, the American transformation how ever is very dramatic from the Haitian and the African Voodoo. This is where the argument begins.

Haitian Voudou is a very complex (as is the common trend of all Voudou) system of spirit organization, the complex combination of Roman Catholicism pushed and forced on to the slave population by the French, as well as some native Taino and Arowak beliefs thrown into the mix. The addition of these native beliefs was the first point of the faith that stands out to as different than as practiced in Benin. The system revolves around 5 major groupings of spirits (though some may say 9 or 7 or many, many more) these spirit nations being Rada, a group of spirits that can be traced back to Dahomey of West Africa, with the exclusion of a few (i.e. the spirit La Sirene). The Djuba, a grouping of almost purely Haitian and Native spirits who preside over agriculture, and prosperity. The Nago, who are predominately Yoruban spirits, the home of all the warrior spirits that can be traced back to Yoruba land. The Petro nation, witch includes Congo, and Haitian spirits, this nation is known for its fiery disposition, and Finally the Gede, the spirits of the ancestral dead, one of the most popular nations of spirits. These spirits all have developed masks of saints and catholic imagery due to the nature of the French, and their demand to take control of the slaves spiritual lives. There are many denominations of Haitian Voodoo but the most popular are Makaya and Hatian Voudou. Makaya witchcraft in some ways may reflect some more African ideas, where we can discover some of the secrets of African bush medicine, as opposed to Voudou witchcraft. It is very religious and spiritual and involves many systems of initiation. So where does this leave us when we compare it to West African Voudou? Only one nation reflects the spirits that they were worshipping, not to mention all the spirits that have been forgotten and are only worshiped in Benin. Dose this difference make it more or less alien than its origins? This evolution of Voudou is how ever very interesting, a system that molded together, to draw a community of estranged people in a foreign land under the totalitarian rule of a foreign nation in order to build a strong community where none are excluded. This is perhaps why their revolution was so successful, where other similar revolts had failed.

Moving on to North America, and in particular New Orleans and most of the Cajun and gulf parishes, there exists a form of Voodoo so unlike Haitian and African Voodoo, so different in fact, that even calling it Voodoo inspires vigorous debate Some say that instead, it belongs to a more spiritual side of Hoodoo, which is more a system of folk magic than a religious system, or that it is just an amalgam of ideas and folklore. But before jumping to conclusions, it's important to look at the common denominator of all of the things both African and Haitian Voodoo has in common. What do the two traditions have in common? Spirits. Some of the names like Papa Legba the spirit of the crossroads, Blanc Dani, the equivalent of the spirit Dambhalla, Joe Feral, the equivalent to Ogou, Cimbee, the equivalent of Simbi a Congo spirit of the sacred waters, and magic, and the very prominent and heavily discussed and debated Le Grand Zombi whose roots can be found in Africa, as well as the mythos surrounding these blessed pythons. These spirits are also revered along side saints, one of the more popular saints is Saint Expedite, to whom they assign many qualities, a personality that is not included in normal Catholic canon. In addition to the spirits, there is a system of folk magic that is intertwined in the tradition called Gris-Gris, or Mojo this is very similar to the Nkisi magic of the Congo. The combination of herbs, stones and biologicals to create a magical talisman is not too dissimilar from the wanga found in Haiti, This is why many critics say that New Orleans Voodoo is nothing more than a branch of Hoodoo. As the spirits fell to disuse and everything relied on the power of ones Conjure man, Root Doctor, Voodoo mama or Voodoo queen, to make a powerful amulet using his or her personal relationship with there own spirits. Of course one can not mention New Orleans Voodoo and not mention that cities Voodoo queen, Marie Laveau. Marie Laveau and her daughter Marie II are known for holding Voodoo rituals in Congo Square and Bayou Saint John. And her most famous ritual the baptism ceremonies at Bayou Saint John on Saint John's day (June 25th). Another aspect of the tradition is found within the spiritualist movement that swept the nation from Buffalo NY, to New Orleans and beyond. In modern days New Orleans Voodoo is commonly associated with drawing in other traditions borrowing from Spiritualism, Santaria, Candomble, Hatian Voodoo, and many other traditions.

So perhaps there is no difference between Hoodoo and New Orleans Voodoo, but does that make the system weaker? New Orleans is and was a rapidly growing city, with many faiths existing amongst one another. They often pick up the other methods from other faiths, as is the tendency of African beliefs but does this corrupt the inherent power? Or make it better or worse than something else? Hoodoo is just as powerful as a system of belief as any of the ones discussed. Is it the use of the word Voodoo? The word means spirit, and all of these faiths have the commonality of all working with and acknowledging spirits. Each system is uniquely unique. And all carry their own weight, and have gone under there own transformations that are all valid, and work well in the hands of the proper people who have used them in the past. Hoodoo country is vast in the United States. As a Practitioner of Voodoo both Hatian and New Orleans, a Root Doctor and conjure man and an amateur anthropologist, I would say that each and every individual division in Voodoo is Voodoo, and that each system is valid on their own and it would be an impossible feat to compare one to the other or what system is actually Voodoo, when the system revolves around nature, and the natural elements, how can we say what is legitimate, or not? Benin Voudou is different than Haitian but is still the natural parent of Hatian Voudou, and New Orleans Voodoo, None are alike, but alas in the end it will be your decision to make. We should come to the understanding that there is not a spirit not worth honoring, some are forgotten or changed as in the case of New Orleans Voodoo, or bid a certain farewell due to safety and security as in the realm of Hatian Voudou. We must never forget the noble roots that this faith comes from, and we must understand again the word "Voudou" means spirit but does not include or exclude any kind of spirits. In this way we should honor all spirits within human reason, which makes all forms of the practice valid.

Joseph Robicheaux is a writer and Occult researcher whose studies focus on traditional societies religious and magical practices lead him to join and practice many traditional paths. A practitioner of Celtic Shamanism, Haitian Vodou, and Brazilian Quimbanda and many other paths, Joseph is also a full time psychic reader and magical advisor at Salem, Massachusetts and North America's oldest Witch supply store Crow Haven Corner.

BLUE BEAM
CONSPIRACY
by Douglas Lain

The trouble with advocates of paranoid awareness, enemies of the control system, dreamers who want to expose the dreamworld, Matrix Warriors who seek to be the one, and all the hordes of practical types who relegate their investigations to the realm of nuts and bolts deep politics is that none of them are quite paranoid enough to understand what's going on. A prime example of the difficulty would be how various conspiracy investigators have dealt with the Blue Beam theory.

What is project Blue Beam? My friend Neil Kramer summed it up in his blog "the Cleaver" this way: "In short, Project Blue Beam is a highly classified black-budget project that takes the application of holographic technology to another level. An integrated array of satellite mounted lasers and ground installations will be used to simulate large-scale religious manifestations and a hostile alien presence. Gods, messiahs, extra terrestrials, motherships – the whole shooting match. Truly a show to *capture the imagination*."

What's going on then is that the government (the real government mind you, not the puppets you see on television) is planning to stage a phony UFO event in order to foist a new religion onto the public and gain complete control of the population, however what's most interesting about this story it how it relies on the presupposition that there have been real UFO landings already. The late William Cooper, for example, was convinced that the government had made a secret pact with ETs, an agreement to allow the aliens to abduct humans in exchange for alien technology. And at the same time he also believed that sometime after 2010 the government would stage a UFO landing on the White House lawn in order to brainwash the public that aliens were real. In fact, Cooper thought that the government would use alien technology in order to pull off the fake UFO stunt, and that the aliens themselves were giving the orders. That is, the big secret was that the fake UFO landing would in fact be orchestrated by real aliens. It would be a fraud that would present a truth in a lie.

If one stops to consider the story it quickly takes on its contradiction. Whatever remains convincing about the Blue Beam conspiracy theory stems only from the deadlock. The possibility that Blue Beam could be true in any conventional or empirical sense dissolves, but we are left with the contradiction at its core. And to continue we have to adopt a sort of dream logic. What is truly strange about the Blue Beam scenario is the way in which this deadlock, this self-contradiction, seems to be endemic not just to conspiracy theories, but also to philosophical systems of epistemology and ontology.

For example, Bishop George Berkeley posited that the world was made entirely of perception. He demonstrated that what we take to be matter, that abstract substance without qualities that provides a substrate for perceived reality, was nothing more than a category mistake. Matter itself was logically impossible. How could something be if it had no way of being? How could something without any perceptible qualities be the source of all perceptions? What Berkeley proved was that matter, in order to be the substrate that supported reality, was impossible. Matter as substance without qualities, an essence without expression, could not be.

The trouble was that, by eliminating matter, Berkeley also exposed at least a methodology for eliminating any and all other substrates. Attempts were made to correct the problem, but in every case the contradiction would reappear. Kant's synthetic apriori, being a contingent fact that was also necessary, is the first example that comes to mind. But there are others.

And if one leaves philosophy behind, if one moves into religion or spirituality, for instance, the impasse is only ignored, but does not disappear. In religion we have Christ who is both God and man at the same time. Or we have a Zen with its universal mind that is also no mind.

When one sees this contradiction, this split between reality and what is perceived, popping up everywhere the temptation is to attempt to reconcile the contradiction by blending the two into one. But this amounts to falling for the conspiracy.

It means accepting that the aliens are among us, but that they are also really a cover story for some other deeper mystery. Or, in the case of philosophy it means abandoning questions of ontology and epistemology and caring only about utilitarian questions. In religion it manifests as believing in God on Sundays, or accepting that neither our perceptions of the world nor our ideas about what lies behind our perceptions are worth a damn. Instead one practices methods and techniques, breathing methods, thinking techniques, to help one remain unattached and uninvolved. With this approach we go along to get along, adopt a tolerance toward everything, meditate, and eat lots of bran.

Blue Beam is a symptom, and as a symptom it is itself out of joint. What needs to be realized is the conspiracy in the conspiracy theory. The self-contradiction, the absurd and phanstastical quality of the story, this is what is most true about Project Blue Beam. And what we need to understand if we're going to get to the bottom of this mystery is what's right there on the surface.

Douglas Lain *was a runner up for the Eliot Fintushel awarad in 2002 but lost out to Eliot Fintushel. His novel* Billy Moon *is forthcoming from Tor Books in August of 2013, and his other books include the short story collection* Fall Into Time *and the novella* Wave of Mutilation, *both from Eraserhead Press.*

Doug is the host of the weekly philosophy podcast Diet Soap.

He is currently working a mystery entitled The Doom that Came to Lolcats, *as well as a nonfiction book entitled* Everything I Ever Needed to Know About Capitalism I Learned from Watching Star Trek.

NEO-ANARCHISM:
A NEW VISION OF
ANARCHY
by Kirk Jones

Many works have sought to forge a connection or generate a conceptual schism between chaos and anarchy. Both endeavors hold equal merit, as they problematize the currently limited understanding—or misunderstanding rather—of what chaos and anarchy can be, and how they function in relation to one another. Perhaps the most ubiquitous misunderstanding is that chaos and anarchy are essentially synonymous. If we ascribe to dichotomous thinking, the belief that chaos and anarchy are synonymous seems reasonable. Chaos, after all, is defined by its dichotomous counterpart, order. Subsequently, anarchy is defined by its opposite, a governmental social order. Since both chaos and anarchy are diametrically opposed by some manifestation of order, it seems practical to place them in the same camp. However, to boil these phenomena down to binary characterization ignores the hierarchy implicit in the relationship between chaos and anarchy. At best, anarchy nestles itself under the umbrella of chaos with several additional catalysts including naturally-occurring forms of chaos as described in the works of James Gleik.

The distinctions between chaos and anarchy do not end there. While chaos is the opposite of order, anarchy represents a breakdown of order. As revolutions of the past have suggested, the breakdown of order requires an equal or greater order and social organization. A new order, in turn, erupts from the eradication of what our forefathers erroneously dubbed natural rights. Only a temporally limited chaos presents itself in anarchy until new orders emerge. These orders, or sub governments, will eventually have to negotiate one another's power until a central or streamlined means of discourse is established. As such, anarchy proves difficult to sustain.

In relation to chaos, anarchy is just as responsible for generating order depending on the means by which anarchy is carried out. In some circumstances, the order in a system of anarchy could easily outweigh the chaos.

Classic understandings of chaos prove equally problematic. Principia Discord, a seminal text on chaos religion, is in itself a fair representation of what a religion based on chaos would appear as. It is paradoxical in its simplicity of content countered by stimulus overload. It is self-contradictory in its call for a religion based upon chaos. It begs interpretation, yet loses its chaotic essence once an interpretation is ascribed to it. To understand the book is to strip it of its chaotic nature, which is perhaps why the book is intentionally setup to evade understanding. Ultimately it says nothing until one ascribes meaning to it, at which point it contradicts the very message it intended to propagate: chaos evades understanding. Chaos only exists in relative form as a breakdown of meaning, which hinges directly upon a person's ability to perceive the world as meaningful and comprehendible information. Our method of understanding hinges upon constructing order through elaborate systems of categorization. We can only grasp chaos by defining it in binaries, i.e. it is predictable in its unpredictability.

From the exploration above, several guiding tenets for neo-anarchism can be derived:

1. Chaos as an end in anarchistic endeavors is sustainably unfeasible, and virtually a paradoxical impossibility. At best, in the context of anarchy chaos is a byproduct that can be minimized or augmented for a limited time.

2. In nearly all contexts, pure chaos is an impossibility. As soon as it springs into existence, new structures emerge and order returns, even if in a meager capacity. Chaos is a fertile ground from which order flourishes.

3. If pure chaos can be achieved, it becomes simultaneously an order in itself. Paradoxically, pure chaos becomes predictable in its unpredictability, definable in that it is indefinable.

The implication of these tenets is that anarchy best serves as a means to an end, which is a newly-established order. There are two means by which this newly-established order can manifest. We can either implement a model in which the level of chaos is minimized during overthrow, or we can implement a model in which the level of chaos is augmented in hopes of reaching a state of pure chaos, from which a new order naturally emerges. Unlike earlier lay manifestations of anarchy, the methodology for implementing these anarchistic variations is rational. The former presents us with a manifestation of anarchy that sustains considerations for human rights. The latter, however, does not. What the latter does is acknowledge the inevitability that those who initiate anarchy are just as likely to perish as those who desperately cling to the old order. I don't present the option as a reality, only a conceptual framework that eradicates the post-apocalyptic survivor fantasy. Striving for pure chaos is necessarily selfless. The misunderstanding that anarchy will somehow act as an objective form of karma—leaving those who perpetuate anarchy to thrive in a new world where those who ascribe to current order will perish at the hands of the disenfranchised—is pitiable at best.

So what is the responsibility of the neo-anarchist? To explore conceptual and real-world applications for anarchy. To usher in a new era of thinking man's anarchism to accompany pop culture notions of anarchy in which chaos and anarchy are ends rather than means, and a rich matrix of connections and concepts is boiled down to a hand-scrawled symbol. Neo-anarchy is a philosophy that is not built upon a necessary destruction of old values, but a new scaffolding parallel to the old understandings of anarchy. It should invite new voices, complications and problematization. Ultimately, what we need is a broadening of perspectives, a non-hierarchical model for all of these perspectives, and venues in which they can thrive equally.

Kirk Jones is the author of the 2010 NBAS title, Uncle Sam's Carnival of Copulating Inanimals. *His work has appeared on* Bizarro Central, Unicorn Knife Fight, *and* Flashes in the Dark. *Stop by and check out his psychotic rants and scathing reviews of children's books at www. bizarrojones.com.*

"What... is real? Are you certain you know what reality is?" —Montag the Magnificent

HERSCHELL GORDON LEWIS'
THE WIZARD OF GORE
(1970)
by Nick Cato

Exploitation film director Herschell Gordon Lewis is the epitome of the old adage "You either love him or hate him." There's simply no way to remain "middle of the road" with any of his films. From his early nudist camp pictures to his first gore film, *Blood Feast* (1963) to his surreal dark fantasy *Something Weird* (1967), all of Lewis' films are plagued (or blessed, depending on your cinematic taste) with horrendous acting, plot holes galore, special effects that were often below amateur level, and editing that was nearly non-existent. And yet Lewis has managed to gain (and maintain) a fan base that's nothing short of amazing.

Among the 37 films Lewis has directed, eight are considered godfathers of the "splatter films" that rose to popularity in the late 70s and early 80s. 1970's *The Wizard of Gore* is easily Lewis' most gruesome offering, and despite the less than convincing FX, there are sequences contained within that are so brutal they border on the absurd.

The Wizard of Gore tells the tale of Montag the Magnificent, a magician who performs vaudeville-type magic shows in front of live audiences. He decapitates himself on stage via guillotine during the first scene in the film, and while you want to laugh at the fake-looking head that rolls onto the stage, the film stock itself makes everything look like some kind of amateur snuff movie. You truly don't know whether to laugh, gag, or pinch yourself to make sure you're not actually having some kind of drug-induced nightmare.

Montag uses hypnosis to get women in the audience to volunteer for his magic tricks. When he has them on stage and under his spell, he ties them up and straps them down, the audience seeing nothing more than a simple illusion. Yet when Montag cuts one poor woman in half with a chainsaw, *we see what Montag sees*: he's actually killing them. Yet, at the end of the trick, the women return to their seats as if nothing has happened. Within a few days, these helpless ladies drop wherever they are and fall apart, proving to be real victims of the onstage crimes. One poor woman is placed under a huge drill press; another has a sword shoved down her throat; yet another has her brains removed after Montag hammers a spike into her head…each "magic trick" more gruesome than the last.

Shelly, an attractive TV talk show host, becomes fascinated with Montag's act, and along with her sports writer-fiancé, Jack, begins to attend his performances. Shelly wants Montag to do his act on her TV program, and he not only agrees, but promises to have a "special treat" in store for her viewers.

That's about as far as the plot goes in *The Wizard of Gore* (but then again, anyone who goes to see something titled *The Wizard of Gore* shouldn't exactly be expecting an intricate plot).

There are a few surreal moments (especially when Montag manages to hypnotize everyone watching the TV show he's on) and some long gab-sessions where even seasoned fans of these types of films might have a hard time not hitting the Fast Forward button. And yet like a nasty car accident, fans of gore films will not be able to look away. The aforementioned drill-press sequence is quite grim. There are no cut-aways from the violence. We see Montag bring the giant press up and down, repeatedly, into the woman's mid-section as blood and guts flow onto the stage in splattery abundance. Lewis always managed to give the audience what they wanted, so no one could ever accuse him of false advertising: in *The Wizard of Gore*, there's more gore and carnage than in most of his other horror films combined.

Even those who are not fans of bad acting have been mesmerized by Ray Sager, the "actor" who plays Montag. With his dull, monotone voice (which he only changes when attempting to accent the last word of each sentence), along with his Halloween-store-looking cape and top hat, he walks around the stage like a young boy who didn't wipe himself good enough during his last visit to the toilet. Even when he works an electric chainsaw, an axe, a sword, or any weapon in his arsenal, he does so with almost no emotion, laughing unconvincingly as he does his ghastly tricks. The couple of times the camera zooms into his eyes as he hypnotizes someone causes more laughs than scares. With all this going against him—we're not afraid of him, we don't buy him as a maniacal slayer of helpless women, we can't stand his voice—there's just something about Ray Sager in the role of Montag the Magnificent that *works*. While I'm assuming your standard horror fan won't last even halfway through of this bloody mess, those of us who have (some, multiple times) credit Sager's non-performance as the highlight of the film . . . even above the outrageous decapitations and amputations. It is one of the best "so-bad-it's-good" roles of all time.

The Wizard of Gore, naturally, is full of so many plot holes and bad edits, you need to sit through it at least 3 times to spot them all. And as far as the "special FX" go, let's just say, despite how nasty the murders are, there aren't too many people out there who are going to be offended by a mannequin head covered in kayro syrup and red food coloring.

And yet . . . this thing still manages to disturb on its own unusual level.

If *The Wizard of Gore* has one positive thing going for it, it's a strong female lead. Sherry Carson (played by Judy Cler—you haven't heard of her before) speaks with authority and knows what she wants. While most of her on-screen time is spent being fascinated by Montag's act, she's not a typical horror-film bimbo. There are a few scenes where she bosses her fiancé Jack around (funny considering he's a he-man sports columnist for a local paper) and talks with a real super-bitch attitude. You'd think in a film where all the victims are female (and for some reason, all are redheads, too), there wouldn't be much pro-feminism. Yet Lewis counteracts the brutality toward the victims with a leading lady who doesn't seem to take anyone's crap.

Jack (played by the nerdy-but-strong-looking Wayne Ratay—you haven't heard of him before, either) gives a decent performance (for a b-movie) and while he suspects all along Montag is responsible—somehow—for all the dead women, he manages to keep his mouth shut until the end, not allowing any potential co-conspirators to get in the way of his hypothesis.

Sherry and Jack are a likeable enough "hero" team, and thanks to Ray Sager's lack of acting skills, come away from this looking like Oscar contenders.

The Wizard of Gore isn't my favorite film from Lewis, but I find it his most memorable. It's goofy, it's ultra-gory, and unlike countless splatter films to follow, it's one of those rare films that, whether you love it or hate it, you never forget.

And *that's* saying something.

Nick Cato *is the author of* Don of the Dead, Antibacterial Pope and Other Incongruous Stories, *and* The Apocalypse of Peter. *He is currently co-authoring a huge volume on 70s occult cinema, and writes the popular 'Suburban Grindhouse Memories' column for* cinemaknifefight.com. *Visit him at nickcato.blogspot.com.*

Artists' Bios

Michael Allen Rose *is a writer, performance artist and musician living in Chicago, IL. You might have seen a book he wrote called* Party Wolves in My Skull. *You might have seen his work in* Phantasmagorium, Kizuna: Fiction for Japan *or at* Every Day Fiction. *You might have seen him outside your window at night, breathing heavily. He also makes music under the name Flood Damage, reads things that are on fire in public, and makes a mean homemade macaroni and cheese. Look for his next book in 2013 and follow his antics at www.MichaelAllenRose.com.*

Daniele Serra *is a professional illustrator. His work has been published in Europe, Australia, United States and Japan, and displayed at various exhibits across the U.S. and Europe. He has worked for DC Comics, Image Comics, Cemetery Dance, Weird Tales magazine, PS Publishing and other publications. He is a winner of the British Fantasy Award.*

Chris Shaw *is an English documentary photographer.*

WITCHCRAFT
IN THE HAREM
ALIYA WHITELEY

'The experience of reading this collection is like being waterboarded by an angel. Shocking, heartbreaking and laugh-out-loud funny, this is some of the best writing I've ever seen. If you like Aimee Bender or Etgar Keret, you will love Witchcraft in the Harem.'
—World Fantasy Award-winner Lavie Tidhar

Witchcraft in the Harem, Aliya Whiteley
RRP: £8.99
ISBN: 9781907133404
136pp.

ND - #0448 - 270225 - C10 - 229/152/7 - PB - 9781907133817 - Gloss Lamination